W9-BQI-670

10 Fascinating Facts About Knights

By Jessica Cohn

Content Consultant
Professor Sarah Peverley
University of Liverpool

Reading Consultant
Jeanne M. Clidas, Ph.D.
Reading Specialist

Children's Press®
An Imprint of Scholastic Inc.

Table of Contents

3

Introduction

The years from 476 to 1500 are called the Middle Ages. Kings and queens were the rulers then. Knights served and protected them. The knights fought many bloody battles. Many later became lords.

Do you want to learn more fascinating facts about the knights in old Europe? Then read on!

Knighthood was a family business

Knights often became lords. They could afford to help their sons become knights.

Knights had to own the best horses, armor, and weapons. That was expensive! This is why the sons of lords had the best chance of becoming knights. Lords were the richest people in the land—after the king, of course!

Girls could not become knights.

But fierce females took part in battles. Joan of Arc is one famous example. She led French troops against the English in 1429. Joan inspired the French to win. And she was just a teenager!

Becoming a knight
took three steps

A page (1) worked his way up to squire (2), then knight (3).

3

2

1

Training for knighthood usually began at age seven. A boy was sent to live at a lord's castle to become a page. He received schooling and fighting lessons.

At 14 or 15 he could progress to being a squire. His lessons became more dangerous! If he proved himself worthy, the young man could become a knight at the age of 21.

A squire had to earn his keep during training. He took care of horses, armor, and weapons for a knight at the castle. He also helped train the pages.

A squire practices fighting on horseback.

"Piggyback" was part of the training

Kids today still play games like these. They ride piggyback and try to knock each other down!

A page was taught to act like a fighter. He learned to swing a wooden sword. He also needed to learn how to ride a horse and fight at the same time. He played piggyback to improve his balance.

It was really helpful! When he became a squire, the boy learned to ride horses using no hands.

Warhorses were taught to fight when young, too. The best horses could kick, trample, and even bite enemy soldiers on command.

Wearing armor was not easy

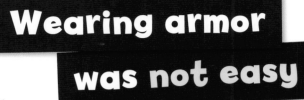

Imagine running around in all this metal!

Learning to wear armor took a while. Knights always needed help getting dressed in their gear. And armor was not easy to wear either! Those plates of metal were heavy! Squires even had to learn how to jump and run while wearing them.

You would not want to wear this on a hot day!

Armor weighed up to 55 pounds. That is like carrying around an eight-year-old! A helmet was up to 8 pounds. It weighed as much as the head it covered!

A knight took his job seriously

The king uses a sword to dub his knight.

To become a knight, a squire had to be **dubbed** in a ceremony. The knight took special vows of **chivalry**.

He promised to protect the weak, obey people in power, and live for honor.

This knight chose blue, yellow, and white for his coat of arms.

Every knight had a coat of arms.

It might have been painted on a shield or sewn onto a banner. The different colors and symbols used on the coat of arms were meant to tell something about the knight. They could symbolize bravery, honesty, loyalty, and more.

Their battle gear was the best

Only knights had armor that was specially made for them.

There were many battles for land and power during the Middle Ages. Sometimes there were not enough knights. Then the townspeople had to help with the fighting, too. Those people could buy cheap armor.

But the best armor was thick and made to fit. That is what knights wore.

Battle horses were also protected by armor. A warhorse had plates of metal to protect its head, neck, and chest.

Even in peacetime, knights kept fighting

Tournaments were great entertainment in the Middle Ages.

In times of peace, knights met for **tournaments**. At these contests, they would **joust** for sport. The warriors would charge at each other at up to 60 miles per hour. That is as fast as a car drives on the highway! They also took part in melees. In these events, teams of knights fought on foot.

The stakes were huge in jousting. Losers lost their horses. They had to give them to the winners.

For a knight, losing a fight also meant losing his horse.

Some helmets had mustaches

As tournaments became more popular, knights would wear fancier gear to joust. Some helmets

People liked to listen to stories and songs about brave knights.

20

airholes

Early helmets protected just the top of a warrior's head. Over the years, knights' helmets were improved. They covered the entire brain and neck. They also had airholes.

The bird on this helmet is made of gold.

had gold on them. Some headgear was decorated with details like mustaches!

Knights and guns did not mix

Kings had paid their knights in different ways. Some knights received money. Many received land instead.

Firearms came into use in Europe in the 1300s. Cannon and guns could stop enemies at a distance and bring down castle walls. Over time, as weapons using gunpowder became more accurate and easier to carry, the need for knights lessened.

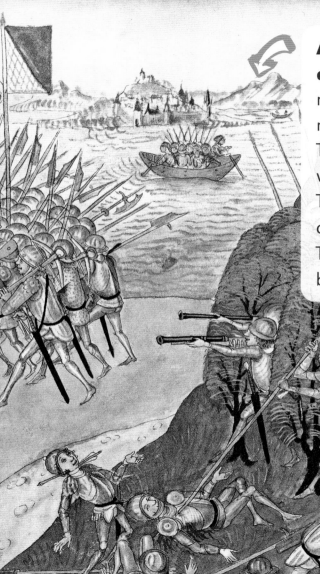

After the 1300s, a king's army might include men-at-arms. These were soldiers who used firearms. There were also archers. They fought with bows and arrows.

Knights still live among us

Steven Spielberg was knighted in 2001.

People still become knights. The royal family of Great Britain gives out knighthoods. But being a knight has a different meaning now. It is an honor for work well done. People who help others may become knights. Inventors may become

knights. Even artists, like Steven Spielberg, become knights. Spielberg directed The BFG and a lot of other movies. Musicians have also been given the honor.

The equivalent of a knighthood for women is a damehood. Helen Mirren, the voice of the dean in Monsters University, was made a dame in 2003.

Activity
Your Own Coat of Arms

Make a coat of arms that shows who you are and what is important to you!

You Will Need:

- ✔ poster board
- ✔ pencil
- ✔ scissors
- ✔ colored pencils, crayons, or markers

1 To make your coat of arms, first pick a shape for your shield.

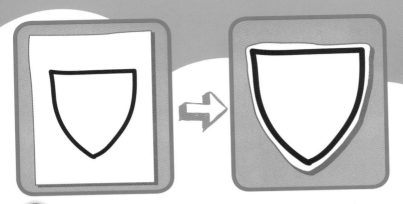

2 Draw the shape on the poster board and cut it out.

3 Add symbols to your shield. You might use a lion to show your strength. Or you might use an owl to represent wisdom.

4 Color in your design. Blue might stand for truth. Green might stand for health. Red might stand for fearlessness.

Timeline

Knights were part of everyday life in the Middle Ages.

The Middle Ages begin in Europe.

5th century ▸ **8th century** ▸ **11th century** ▸ **12th century**

The first knights serve a ruler in western Europe called Charlemagne.

Knights in France begin wearing coverings made of mail to protect their arms, legs, and body.

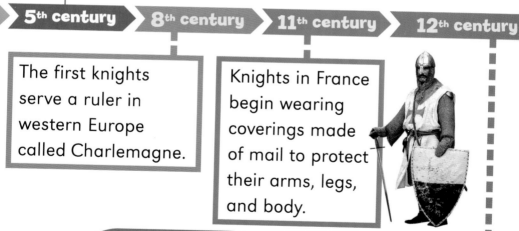

A group of stories are written about King Arthur, his knights, and a kingdom called Camelot.

The first firearms come into use across Europe.

The Middle Ages end in Europe. The need for knights ends.

People try, with little success, to make bulletproof armor.

13th century **14th century** **15th century** **16th century**

Knights begin to cover their bodies with plates of metal.

Glossary

- **chivalry** (SHIV-uhl-ree): code of noble and polite behavior that was expected of a knight in the Middle Ages

- **dubbed** (DUBD): named or declared someone ready, such as being ready to be a knight

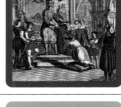

- **joust** (JOWST): compete on horseback with lances

- **tournaments** (TOOR-nuh-muhnts): series of contests in which a number of people or teams try to win the championship

About the Author

Jessica Cohn lives in California with her family. She enjoys hiking, helping student writers, writing books like this one, and exploring. She says that if she had to pick one symbol for her own knightly shield, it might be a big eye. There is so much to see and learn!

Facts for Now

Visit this Scholastic Web site for
more information on knights:
www.factsfornow.scholastic.com
Enter the keyword **Knights**

Library of Congress Cataloging-in-Publication Data

Title: 10 fascinating facts about knights/by Jessica Cohn.

Other titles: Ten fascinating facts about knights

Description: New York: Children's Press, an imprint of Scholastic Inc., [2017]
| Series: Rookie star fact finder | Includes index.

Identifiers: LCCN 2016030339| ISBN 9780531222614 (library binding)
| ISBN 9780531226773 (pbk.)

Subjects: LCSH: Knights and knighthood—Juvenile literature

Classification: LCC CR4513 .C635 2017 | DDC 940.—dc23 LC record available at https://lccn.loc.gov/2016030339

Produced by Spooky Cheetah Press
Design by Judith Christ-Lafond

© 2017 by Scholastic Inc.

Photographs ©: cover: Scott Campbell/Alamy Images; cover background, back cover background: stock09/Shutterstock, Inc.; back cover: Distrikt 3/Shutterstock, Inc.; 2: Sibrikov Valery/Shutterstock, Inc.; 3 left: DEA/C. Balossini/Getty Images; 3 right: FXQuadro/Shutterstock, Inc.; 4 shield: St. Nick/Shutterstock, Inc.; 4-5 background: St. Nick/Shutterstock, Inc.; 4 background: Andrey_Kuzmin/Shutterstock, Inc.; 5 boy: Guryanov Andrey/Shutterstock, Inc.; 6: The Granger Collection; 7: Time Life Pictures/Getty Images; 8: Paris Pierce/Alamy Images; 9: Universal History Archive/UIG/Getty Images; 10 bottom left: Florilegius/SSPL/Getty Images; 10 right, 11: al_papito/Shutterstock, Inc.; 12: crazycolors/Fotolia; 13 scale: bikeriderlondon/Shutterstock, Inc.; 13 helmet: Distrikt 3/Shutterstock, Inc.; 13 boy: Littlekidmoment/Shutterstock, Inc.; 14: Florilegius/SSPL/Getty Images; 15: FXQuadro/Shutterstock, Inc.; 16: withGod/Shutterstock, Inc.; 17: withGod/Shutterstock, Inc.; 18: Leemage/UIG/Getty Images; 19: arfo/iStockphoto; 20: Prisma Archivo/Alamy Images; 21 bottom right: DEA/A. Dagli Orti/Getty Images; 21 top left: Sibrikov Valery/Shutterstock, Inc.; 22: kapyos/Shutterstock, Inc.; 23: Soldiers armed with guns, lances and crossbows, from the Berner Chronik, by Diebold Schilling the Elder (c.1445-85) 1483 (vellum), Swiss School, (15th century)/Private Collection/Bridgeman Art Library; 24: Marshall/Ron Sachs/Newsmakers/Getty Images; 25 left: Fiona Hanson/AFP/Getty Images; 25 right: Photos 12/Alamy Images; 26-27 illustrations: Keith Plechaty; 26 boy: Erik Isakson/Media Bakery; 28 top: Heriateg Images/Getty Images; 28 bottom left: DEA/J.E. Bulloz/Getty Images; 28 bottom right: DEA/C. Balossini/Getty Images; 29 top: Alain Marchet (3)/Alamy Images; 29 bottom: Henning Mertens/iStockphoto; 30 top: Ivy Close Images/Alamy Images; 30 center bottom: Robert Creigh/iStockphoto; 30 center top: Florilegius/SSPL/Getty Images; 30 bottom: Leemage/UIG/Getty Images.

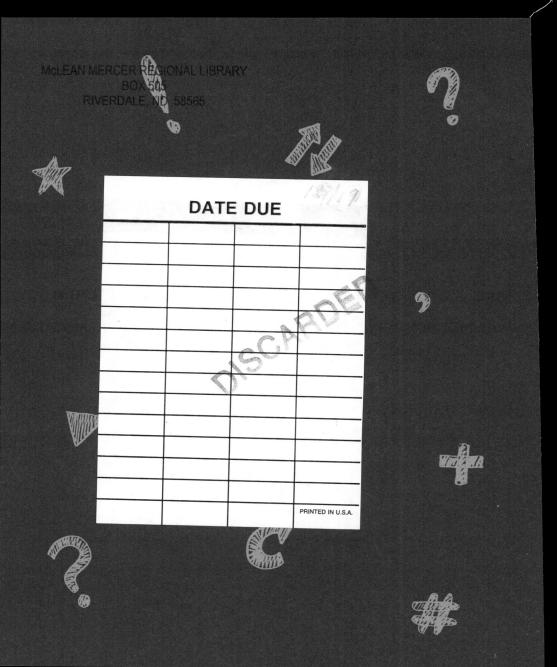

DATE DUE

PRINTED IN U.S.A.